NASCAR Champions

DALE EARNHARDT JR.

Nicole Pristash

PowerKiDS press™

New York

Published in 2009 by The Rosen Publishing Group, Inc.
29 East 21st Street, New York, NY 10010

First Edition

Book Design: Michael J. Flynn
Layout Design: Kate Laczynski
Photo Researcher: Jessica Gerweck

Photo Credits: All images © Getty Images.

Library of Congress Cataloging-in-Publication Data

Pristash, Nicole.
   Dale Earnhardt Jr. / Nicole Pristash. — 1st ed.
        p. cm. — (NASCAR champions)
   Includes index.
   ISBN 978-1-4042-4445-0 (library binding)   ISBN 978-1-4042-4541-9 (pbk)
   ISBN 978-1-4042-4559-4 (6-pack)
   1. Earnhardt, Dale, Jr.—Juvenile literature. 2. Automobile racing drivers—United States—Biography—Juvenile literature. I. Title.
   GV1032.E19P75 2009
   796.72092—dc22
   [B]
                                         2007046647

Manufactured in the United States of America

Contents

Dale Earnhardt Jr. is a NASCAR driver, just like his father Dale Earnhardt.

4

5

When he was young, Dale Jr. worked as a **mechanic**. He and his brother built their own race car and Dale began racing.

6

At 22, Dale Earnhardt Jr. started racing in the Busch **Series**. He became the **champion** in 1998 and 1999.

8

For the Nextel Cup Series, Dale drove a car with the number eight on it. It is the same number his father and grandfather once used.

Dale Jr. often **competed** against his father. His father drove a car with the number three on it.

13

In 2001, Dale Jr.'s father passed away. Dale kept racing, though. He even finished in eighth place in the **rankings** that year.

14

Dale Jr. pushed forward. In 2004, he won the Daytona 500. This is one of NASCAR's most **popular** races.

Off the track, Dale likes to sign **autographs** for his fans.

18

In 2008, Dale Jr. changed teams. His new number is 88. Dale hopes to become champion of the Sprint Cup Series.

Glossary

autographs (AH-toh-grafs) A person's name, written by that person.

champion (CHAM-pee-un) The best, or the winner.

competed (kum-PEET-ed) To have gone against another in a game or test.

mechanic (mih-KA-nik) A person who is good at fixing cars.

popular (PAH-pyuh-lur) Liked by lots of people.

rankings (RAN-kingz) Guides to how well a player is doing in a sport.

series (SIR-eez) A group of races.

22

Books and Web Sites

Books

Kelley, K.C. *NASCAR: Racing to the Finish*. Pleasantville, NY: Reader's Digest, 2005.

Schaefer, Adam R. *The Daytona 500*. Mankato, MN: Coughlan Publishing, 2004.

Web Sites

Due to the changing nature of Internet links, the Rosen Publishing Group, Inc., has developed an online list of Web sites related to the subject of this book. This site is updated regularly. Please use this link to access the list: www.powerkidslinks.com/nascar/dalejr/

Index